M000029220

SPECIALLY WRAPPED GIFTS

A Mother's Journey into the Unexpected World of Disability

Unless otherwise indicated, Scripture quotations are taken from the New International Version (NIV).

First Edition: 2019

Cover Design and Interior Layout by Yvonne Pierre
Edited by Christina Jodoin
Photographs by Rachel Davis

Specially Wrapped Gifts is a 501(c) (3) non-profit organization registered in the state of Tennessee. The purpose is to demonstrate the love of Christ to families affected by special health needs and/or disabilities by providing encouragement and resources.

Website: Speciallywrappedgifts.org
Facebook: Specially Wrapped Gifts Ministry
Contact: Speciallywrappedgifts14@gmail.com
Periscope: shemekacherryjackson

SPECIALLY WRAPPED GIFTS

A Mother's Journey into the Unexpected World of Disability

Shemeka Cherry Jackson

2019

FOREWORD

I met Shemeka over 20 years ago while serving in the Navy. She was assigned to my unit. One thing that stood out to me, even as a young Sailor, was her sensitivity to God and her desire to encourage others and give hope. It is no surprise to me that Shemeka Cherry Jackson, my friend, and spiritual sister, would take an event in life that would devastate, destroy or put in mental constraints any mother and bring forth positivity.

If there is a problem, there is a solution. With a very compassionate heart, this is how she has faced life and situations, not only for herself but also for others. To find out how to navigate through life with compassion and purpose has always been a driving force for Shemeka.

When she called to inform me about Candace, of course, the first thing was to be a listening ear. I thought I would hear devastation, the "why's"; but instead, I heard how God was going to get them through it and how so much she wanted to reach out to others that were going through the same thing.

Then I got a phone call about starting Specially Wrapped Gifts. Again, no surprise to me, so I sowed a seed into this special ministry.

This book will give you the courage to face whatever situation with God's grace, God's love and God's presence. I pray this book will be available in all hospitals, to all Mothers, letting them know they have a Specially Wrapped Gift, and that love conquers all.

Evangelist H. Ann Kimble
RPCS(SW), USN (Ret)
Jacksonville, Florida
Mentor, Evangelist, Spiritual Mother
evangelistkimble@msn.com

REVIEWS

"As a certified occupational therapy assistant and a parent with a special needs child, I have witnessed several outstanding advocates. Through Shemeka's ministry, Specially Wrapped Gifts, she has shown parents how to be great advocates for their children. This book will be a great read for anyone who is trusting God for guidance with their special needs child."

-Bridgette Joy, a parent of an adult child with Down syndrome, certified OTA, Memphis, TN

"This book is not only going to help parents/families with raising a child with special needs, but it spoke to me about the love and faithfulness of God!"

-Kesha, mom of 3, Oak Ridge, TN

"I moved to Oak Ridge, TN in 2011 and my son, Pierre (autism spectrum), was having a very hard time adjusting in school. His occupational therapist suggested a support group where I could be with other parents of special needs children; where I could vent while allowing Pierre the opportunity to bond and make friendships. I never would have considered that I too would connect and grow close and bonded with the members of the group, but I did.

My faith in God allowed me to get through the hard times and I thank Him for allowing others to come into our lives to where a difference was made on both sides. Shemeka is dedicated, hard-working, and extremely loving towards her girls and encouraged Candace (like she did Cherie) to soar and be her best self. I encourage all parents of children with special needs to do the same because our children are worth it."

-Denise Conner, mother of a son on the autism spectrum, Oak Ridge, TN

Shemeka is My God- Sent Sister for over 23 years, friend and leader in all aspects. Shemeka has been there and prayed me through some tough times of my life and some of my greatest accomplishments. Please allow her walk with God and this book to speak to your spirit and help you to build a Greater relationship with God. Blessings...

-LaKecia Shuman, Jacksonville, FL

"In this book, Shemeka gives a personal account of her feelings, experiences, and challenges as a mother of a daughter with special health needs. I, too, can relate as I share the same story. Thank you for being a voice for our community. Your words are encouraging, motivating, and inspiring. This book gives me comfort in knowing that I'm not alone on my journey. You are truly a blessing!

-Tawanna F. Reid, mother of two,

Knoxville, TN

SPECIALLY WRAPPED GIFTS

A Mother's Journey into the Unexpected
World of Disability

TABLE OF
CONTENTS

ONE

TO WHOM MUCH IS
GIVEN

Luke 12:48
From everyone who has been given much,
much will be demanded; and from the one
who has been entrusted with much, much
more will be asked.

A Diamond in the Rough

Only after spending time with someone do we get to know their character and trust their heart. My relationship with God began when I was seven years old. I became a born-again Christian, believing that Jesus died on the cross for my sins and rose from the grave, asking Him into my heart and for the forgiveness of my sins.

For many people, they come to know the Lord after they have tried everything else. We hear powerful testimonies of how God delivered someone from drugs or alcohol and on and on. That was not my experience. For me, getting saved at seven was more 'preventative maintenance' so that I would not have to experience that lifestyle.

I grew up in the inner-city of Chicago, Illinois. Humboldt Park Neighborhood: a predominantly Puerto Rican neighborhood, which was full of life, culture, delicious foods, music, and festivals, was also ridden with drugs, poverty and gang violence. Growing up in the city made me resilient, street savvy, and well-rounded. My mother was a single parent raising three kids. My parents were never married to each other and were teenagers when I was born. My grandmother played a major role in my life because my mother was a young mom.

This was not unusual in my neighborhood: single parents or children being raised by grandparents were common. Most of my close friends did not grow up with their father in the home. I saw parents that wanted their children to have the world, be successful, finish school, join the military and go on to have successful careers, but they had limited knowledge about how to make that happen.

As kids, we have dreams of college, careers or the military, but if you do not see that or have a guide to show you how to get there, those dreams can die because of the overwhelming frustration or lack of guidance. I would imagine in most communities, graduating high school was a normal expectation. In my neighborhood, it was a *big* deal, because there were so many distractions along the way: high school dropouts, teen pregnancy, joining a gang, crime, and violence. For me, I wanted to do more and be more. I wanted to go to college and break the cycle of poverty in my own life. I did not know how I would make that happen, but I had an instinct that I was made for *more*.

My drive to accomplish more and make an impact in my family and in the world was affirmed because I had a glimpse of what my future could be and would be. My everyday surroundings were poverty, but that was not all I saw. Having a window outside of my community painted pictures for me— cast vision and gave me hope. Exposure expanded my horizon to different walks of life. Primarily, because we attended a multicultural church. This church was multi-cultural not only in race but socioeconomically, backgrounds, experiences, age, and gender. At both the private school I attended and, in my church, we would have missionaries from overseas come and talk about life in Africa, the

Philippines, and Columbia, just to name a few. Our church would sing worship songs in Spanish and learned a tune in Swahili. We had a World's Fair potluck dinner once a year at our church to celebrate the diversity in our congregation.

I remember that my grandmother, who lived across the street from us, was intentional in taking us on road trips and seeing different ways of life. She would host backyard Bible club in our neighborhood, have Friday night Bible studies with me and my peers, and took us to summer camp. Some parents in our neighborhood struggled to feed their children and keep a roof over their heads. It was not unusual for us to have strangers over for dinner. I remember us giving out Thanksgiving baskets to families that needed them. We would host Christmas parties and give away nice gifts, toys, games, and of course the boring stuff: socks, underwear, and t-shirts to the families in our neighborhood. My grandmother would partner with churches from the suburbs or families in our church that were better off than we were and invite them to spend a day with a child in her Bible Study. I enjoyed this. I remember a family that I was paired with lived in a beautiful high-rise in downtown Chicago. Their neighbors were friends with players from the Chicago Cubs baseball team. Through them, I was able to meet Andre Dawson and Ryne Sandburg, creating a lasting impression on me. Most of these experiences came through church or Bible Study, so, to me, that was the Body of Christ-- working together, having fun, and doing life together.

This was my neighborhood and I felt like I had the best of both worlds. I was a young girl, raised in the church, attended a private Christian school for my elementary years, and had a sensitivity to God. I also could see and feel despair. I could relate and identify with those around me, but in a lot of ways, I felt shielded, not having to go through a lot of it personally. We were blessed in the sense that I grew up in a house with a lot of love. My mother and grandmother were vocal and intentional to let me know that. I had a lot of love from my father's side of the family as well and recall fond memories of spending time with my father, my grandmother, and cousins. We did not have the worry of where our next meal was coming from, but not everyone in my neighborhood could say that. This was a gift, because God, through my upbringing, instilled in me a sensitivity to people that might feel marginalized.

These early experiences helped to lay a foundation and teach me about God's character. We are His representation and He will often use people to create a miracle for someone else. In the Kingdom of God, there is no class system, He cares just as much for the poor as He does for the rich. "God is not a respecter of persons" (Acts 10:34), he does not show partiality because of a person's race or economic status.

After high school, I knew that I wanted to serve my country, so I enlisted in the Navy when I was 17 years old. I served for four years. I felt proud to be on my own. I would decide if I wanted to continue in the church and make my own decisions, and through that, learn to trust God for myself. Up until this point, I had my mother, grandmother, family, and church family that was protection for me, but I had to learn to pray my own prayers and have my own walk—experience God for myself. God had invested much in me at an early age. Selecting me, He opened doors for me that had been closed to others in similar situations. I could only wonder what the return on His investment would entail.

Ordering My Steps

After boot camp, I joined the fleet, observed various positions, and then was able to apply for a job that interested me. Like I mentioned, I had grown up in church and honestly felt tired of it and wanted a break from it. I was proud to serve my country and joining the Navy gave me just enough legroom between me and God. I could figure things out for myself and develop my own relationship. My duty station was at a Naval Air station and my job was to put up the flight schedule and help on the flight line.

I enjoyed doing that. Here I was, from inner-city Chicago, serving my country.

I'm not sure how this conversation came about, but a fellow shipmate suggested that I apply for the open position at the chapel. *Working at the chapel is an actual job in the Navy?* I am certain that God has a sense of humor and His plans will prevail in the end. I applied and was interviewed by one of the chaplains and was selected for the position. I was a "Religious Program Specialist" which in layman's terms is a Chaplain's Assistant. Chaplains are non-combatants so they do not carry weapons. Oftentimes, others do not think of the Chaplain until they need to. For some people, they represent God, for others, they bring hope and encouragement. Chaplains serve as a safe place and their presence boosts troop morale.

I loved it. It was a mix of religion, philosophy, and compassion. We met Sailors and Marines where they were, without judgment. Human beings have an innate knowing that we are a part of and connected to something greater than ourselves.

My role in the military supported U.S Constitution, Freedom of Religion. I assisted in creating access and provided support for Sailors and Marines to worship in their own expression.

I worked for Protestant, Seventh Day Adventist, Jewish, and Catholic Chaplains. I put together the religious services, Jewish Seder meals, Sunday School classes, mid-day mass, funeral services, and weddings. I ordered supplies, liturgical dress, created church bulletins, cleaned baptisteries—you name it. On rare occasions, I would travel with the Chaplain to deliver a Red Cross message to a Sailor or Marine. The times that I was able to accompany, it was to deliver a message about the death of a loved one back home. I gravitated to the idea of using faith to bring comfort to people in these moments.

There is an adage, "There are no atheists in foxholes." What I understand that to mean is that we will all encounter a crisis of belief. There will be a pivotal moment in our life that will cause us to seek answers to existential questions, even if up to that point, you did not have a need to. Oftentimes, in the face of tragedy or death we seek to solve the deep mystery: *Why? How could this happen?* The idea of a 'foxhole'—combat, war, and the enemy are coming at you. You must defend yourself: kill or be killed. At that moment, you are going to hope there is a God and cry out for help.

Although the chapel was a government building, it was a sacred place. Everybody had equal access to pray, sing, and express their faith. What touched me most was that we were on a military base, training for war and surrounded by weapons and heavy artillery. The chapel was the only place you put down your arms. You surrendered to someone Higher—a greater authority. Weapons were not allowed in the chapel. The chapel was Holy ground, and regardless of the faith, there was reverence and fear of God. In this space He talks, you listen. You submit. You quiet your soul and let His presence quell all worries, fears, and distractions.

After my enlistment in the Navy, I moved back to Chicago to attend college. That was important for me because I would be the first one in my family to go to college. I chose to major in Psychology because I always had an interest in human behavior. I have always been drawn to those topics, whether reading or conversations. Not only was that interesting to me, but I wondered if other people were drawn to me for that as well. I would often joke, that I have "I like to listen. I want to help" etched in invisible ink on my forehead because it never fails: for some reason, that person who needed someone to talk to or advice on a deeply personal situation would always find me. I would often find myself having a deeply personal conversation with someone I had just met.

Although my major was Psychology and my minor was in Women's Studies, I felt the reoccurring theme, "Why do I believe what I believe?" In the humanistic environment that college tends to be, I was being challenged to give an answer for things I had learned to accept by faith about the Bible, religion, and God. *Apologetics* has the root word "apology", not in the sense of "I am sorry," but more of a defense of why you believe what you believe. This process of learning apologetics sharpened my critical thinking skills and strengthened my faith.

TWO

FINDING THE
PERFECT GIFT

James 1:17
*Every good and perfect gift is from above,
coming down from the Father of the
heavenly lights, who does not change like
shifting shadows.*

I must admit that I am not a big shopper. I am that person who will put off gift buying until the last minute, having to settle on a gift card. For some people, a gift card is a perfect gift because they can purchase what they want in the perfect size and color. For others, they want a selected and purposeful gift. For myself, I prefer personal gifts. I know, the *nerve*. I appreciate gift cards, but when someone selects a gift just for me, it is special. Who doesn't appreciate that? Some people are great gift-givers. My husband, Bruce, gives wonderful gifts, and he is well known for it. It is to the point that when we have a family 'grab bag,' family members hope that Bruce selects their name. His gifts are personal, unique to the receiver, and valuable. He has a good eye for quality and fashion. Bruce enjoys watching people open the gifts he gives; the way their eyes light up and acknowledge, "How did you know? This is just what I wanted! I love it."

When I think about my husband and his love for gift-giving, I imagine that God must be the same way—how He enjoys giving His children good gifts! The verse mentioned at the beginning of the chapter speaks, not only of God's love for gift-giving but also that all of His gifts are good, beneficial and have intrinsic value. His gifts are not haphazard, random, thrown together, rock-bottom cost or low-end quality. They are personal and unique. This verse also speaks to His character. God's character never changes, but when life happens, or we experience unexpected situations that we do not understand, pain or loss, we cannot help but ask "Why?"

In our humanness, we cannot understand why a good God who gives good gifts would allow these things to happen to us. In this disconnect between a good God and our negative experiences, we search for resolution and, often, for someone or something to blame. We demand answers to situations that are a mystery and out of our control. When life throws a curve-ball, we can be encouraged by this verse to remember God's character, that He is good and that He can be trusted.

Such a Good Father

After graduating from college, I visited my mother and siblings in Tennessee. During that time, I decided to apply for a job, just to see what happened. I applied for a case manager position at a social service agency in Tennessee. Right after my interview, I met a man named Bruce on the elevator who would later become my husband. I am so glad I decided to apply for that job. God knew exactly what He was orchestrating in my life. I had no idea at the time all of the things he had in store for us. I was hired for the position! As it turned out, Bruce and I were both from Chicago. Bruce had already lived in Knoxville for a few years after he had relocated here for college. We were both case managers for families at risk of foster care placement or juvenile court intervention. We connected vulnerable families with valuable community resources, whether it was housing, food, job training, and/or facilitating

parenting classes, budgeting, or life skills. Bruce
facilitated an anger management group for school-
age boys and I facilitated a self-esteem group for
girls.

We had hearts for the vulnerable,
marginalized, and oppressed. Through our work,
God knit our hearts together and allowed us to get to
know each other, fall in love, and really focus on our
values and how we wanted to live our lives. I
admired Bruce's commitment to family and our
shared views on our Christian faith, roles of family,
and raising children. I loved our shared passions,
(and it helped that he was *fine*, tall, dark, and
handsome). Bruce was also playing professional
indoor football at the time. He was 350lb and 6'2":
not someone you would want to meet in a dark alley,
but at the same time, he was a gentle giant. He is the
type who wants all the details. For example, if
someone had a new baby, he would be the one to
ask, "How much did the baby weigh? How long is
it?" He has a deep sensitivity to other people's
needs. When I met him, Bruce told me how, even

though he had grown up in church, had only recently asked the Lord into his life to be his Lord and savior. He was actively involved in his church and community, including knocking on doors and inviting people to church and evangelizing to them. Bruce started to attend a small group at the church I was attending. This group of friends challenged us, held us accountable, and helped us to grow in the Lord and with each other.

Bruce already had a son, BJ, and I admired his commitment to him. Bruce was considering pursuing other career opportunities, but most would involve relocating. With each opportunity he had, he always filtered it through the lens of "will this compromise my role of being a father to my son?" He wanted to always be around for him and have an active role in parenting him. This made me admire him even more. I appreciated the lessons that he was giving, and how he valued hard work, church, loyalty, and finishing what you start. BJ looked up to his father and Bruce did not take it lightly that he had BJ's attention. BJ would spend the weekends with us even after we got married. My role was to be an extra layer of support to show love and provide guidance and encouragement.

I had so many insecurities and questions about marriage. I did not grow up in a house where my parents were married. My grandmother had never married, and my mother did not get married until I was 17 years old. I knew about the roles in marriage and had concepts of what this would look like, but did not really see it up close. Bruce and I went through pre-marital counseling and it was great preparation. I had a lot of distorted ideas about marriage and my role. *Can I continue to have my opinions and identity?* Bruce, on the other hand, grew up with both of his parents. He is the third of six children, whereas I am the oldest of my mother's children and the oldest of my father's children.

A New Legacy

I knew that our family would be special because we were starting a new legacy. After one year of marriage, we found out that I was pregnant with our daughter, Cherie. Cherie would be the first one on my side of the family that was born in marriage. Growing up in a Christian environment helped to shape my perspective on family and gave me a different vision for how I wanted to live. My plan was to return to work right away, but when I first held her, I thought, "*Who would I trust you with? God has entrusted you to me.*" My pregnancy with Cherie was normal; I had her at 39 weeks. She was nine pounds and 21 ½ inches long.

After I met Cherie, my desires had changed. Rather than wanting to return to work, my desire was to stay home or work a flexible schedule so I could have the most direct impact on Cherie's life. I had a desire for her to learn sign language, not only for communication but also because I wanted her to know that there are other people in the world who are different from her. For some odd reason, I wanted her to have friends with special needs. During her early years, we enrolled Cherie in a program from birth to kindergarten and I purchased videos so that we could learn basic sign language together. Cherie was very smart and caught on quickly. She was advanced for her age.

After having Cherie, Bruce and I knew that we wanted to have another child. When I found out that I was pregnant with our second, we were excited to welcome another life into the world. I thought I would like to have a boy since we already had a girl; and this time, I planned to return to work. Besides, God gives us the desires of our heart, right? However, we found out that we were, in fact, having another girl. During the pregnancy, we didn't have anything to be alarmed about. We knew that I would have another C-section since I had one with Cherie. When I delivered, I would be 31 years old. My pregnancy was pretty routine, including morning sickness. My amniotic fluids were low towards the end of my pregnancy and Candace did not move much. I had to do a kick-count after I ate. This was a contrast for Cherie, who was full of energy especially when I was trying to rest. My blood pressure started to elevate as my pregnancy progressed and the doctor recommended bed rest and a stress test. Given these factors, my OBGYN doctor thought it would be best for us to deliver at 37 weeks, so we scheduled my C-section for October 28, 2008.

Choosing a Name

God knows our names even before our parents name us. This is refreshing to me because my name is Shemeka. This is not the type of name you can easily find on a coffee mug or key chain. I remember field trips and my classmates being able to find their name, but I never could. Shemeka is unique. I would appreciate it as I got older. My mother always insisted on spelling my name "Shemeka." Now, Shemeka can be spelled many ways, but my mother insisted on this particular spelling. Later in life, I had an interesting encounter with a Jewish Rabbi and he caught the spelling of my name. Not only was Noah's son named *Shem* (Genesis 10:1), but God's name is "Holy" and traditionally Jewish people do not speak it but will refer to God as *HaShem* "The

Name" in substitution for God's formal name *Adonai* meaning "My Master." I don't know what all this means but it blessed me that God is so meticulous even about the way words are spelled.

We had decided on the name Candace early in the pregnancy. Bruce was particularly fond of the name and we thought it was cute to have both a Candace and Cherie. Cherie is spin off my maiden name, Cherry. We chose to spell it Cherie, which is French for "my love", but we still pronounce it "Cherry." We had yet to settle on a middle name for Candace, even up to the point of checking into the hospital. While waiting to be taken back to the operating room, Bruce said, "Her middle name should be Micah, that's what God told me this morning while I was in the shower." God speaks to us even about what we should name our children. Do you believe that? He wants to be intimately involved in our worlds. If He cares what we name our children, don't you think he cares about the details of our lives? I think of Matthew 6:26, "Look at the birds of the air; they do not sow or reap or store away in barns, and yet your heavenly Father feeds them. Are you not much more valuable than they?"

Ok! Her name will be Candace Micah Jackson. I thought it sounded cute. You see, my nickname is Meka so Micah has a similar sound. We had considered Micah early in the pregnancy, but it didn't fit at the time. I didn't have a reference or purpose for it, other than the way it sounded. I know that God does things for a reason, so why so specific in what we named her? *What does the name Micah even mean?* I wondered. The name Micah means, "Who is like Yahweh?" Micah 6:8 "He has shown you, O mortal, what is good, and what the Lord requires of you? To act justly, and to love mercy, and to walk humbly with your God." Wow! Micah was an Old Testament prophet, whose frustrations and messages were a chastisement of the rich, powerful and elite for their mistreatment of the poor, marginalized, outcasts and vulnerable. He cared for those in society who did not have a voice. God saw their plight, heard their cries and was concerned about the 'least of these' (Matthew 25:40). I would come to learn that this bidding question was an invitation to know Him more and to worship Him despite my questions and circumstances. Nothing and no one compares to Him and God wanted me to experience this aspect of His character for myself. *Who is like God?* A rhetorical question that my soul needed to answer but my answer would only come from experience. I have hung onto that question throughout my sweet daughter's life.

Bruce and I went back to the operating room, the anesthesiologist gave me the epidural, and the doctor started to cut. He couldn't believe that I could feel him cutting. In his eight years of experience, no one had been able to feel anything. He decided to put me to sleep. At that point, Bruce was asked to wait in the room, since I would be asleep during the surgery.

While I was asleep, Bruce recalled the events that took place to me later. I was sitting in the room watching the television and the nurse came quickly down the hall with Candace. Bruce remembers the medical team flying down the hall and beckoning for him to go with them. Candace was blue and in respiratory distress. She needed to be transported to Children's Hospital.

When I finally did wake up in recovery, I could sense something was unusual. My mother, stepfather, and hospital nurses were all in the room-- but not Candace. My husband came in and collapsed in the rocking chair next to me sobbing uncontrollably. I was afraid and started to cry, "*I can't take this.*" By this time, the Neonatal Intensive Care Nurse from Children's Hospital had come in. All I wanted to know was *is she alive? Just answer that.* She was alive! That was all I needed to know, anything else I felt like I could handle.

The nurse explained that they needed to take her to the Children's Hospital because she was having difficulty breathing and was in distress. I just wanted to see my daughter before they took her. After I had moved back into my room, the nurse brought Candace in. She was in the incubator so I couldn't touch her. I couldn't hold her, but I desperately wanted to. I felt like she wanted her mommy and I wanted her. I was afraid and could only imagine that she was too. She was being taken from her safe place in my womb, from my voice, my heartbeat and my scent to somewhere completely foreign; to bright lights, strange voices, and people, to a sterile and artificial environment. I was only able to see her. She was so beautiful and perfect, with a full head of hair- *that explains the heartburn during my pregnancy...* The nurses had put a pink bow on her hair and asked if I planned to breastfeed, which I did. They provided me a baby blanket to sleep with so that Candace could recognize my scent, and a breast pump to start pumping milk for them to feed her.

She was being transported to Children's Hospital. Children's Hospital is downtown, while I was across town, about 20 minutes away. I had to let her go. Keeping her with me was not an option. She needed to go because her life hung in the balance and I couldn't do anything. At that moment, I had a choice: to fear for my baby or to trust God. As I saw them take her away, a rush of thoughts came to my mind: *What was she thinking? Was she afraid? Would they take care of her?*

You prepare so much while you carry a child. There are so many sweet memories even during pregnancy, like feeling their first kick, or someone noticing your baby bump, and the excitement of telling family and friends. During both pregnancies, I would play music for my children. Bruce and I would lay hands on my belly and speak over their lives and talk about the awesome plans that God had in store for them. We would talk about how excited we were to meet them and how blessed we were to have them. We would daydream about things that they would like to do. Cherie would be beautiful and smart with long, thick hair. Bruce wondered whether she would be a "southpaw" (left-handed). If so, she could play first base. *Really?* I knew that this was reminiscent of his love for baseball. Don't all parents do that as they anticipate their babies? It may seem silly, but you cannot help but think up these things. We knew that Candace would be a girl and had big dreams for her as well. I imagined that she would have thick hair, great for ponytails and barrettes. She would be smart and confident. I wondered about sibling rivalry, the girls would share a bedroom, after all. Would they enjoy being dressed alike? Bruce would rub my belly and speak over their lives, of God's plans for them. I would play music and read stories. They were welcome here and we were excited about meeting both girls.

As Candace was on the other side of town fighting for her life, Bruce had already called our family in Chicago to tell them the news and my mother had our church family, friends and other people praying. I knew intercessors who knew how to reach the heart of God and I called them to pray for our Candace Micah- *Who is like God?*

One of the nurses from Children's Hospital called and updated us that Candace had arrived, and they were taking good care of her. *Praise God!* While back at the hospital, Bruce, my mother and my stepfather Greg, were eerily quiet. I felt there was something more. My mother and Greg had stepped out, leaving me and Bruce alone to talk. Bruce opened up to tell me that the nurse said Candace had features that led them to believe that she had Down syndrome- almond-shaped eyes, excess skin at the back of her neck, and short pinkies. My bewildered husband attempted to make sense out of what he had heard, but it was all so overwhelming. He tried reasoning with the nurses, explaining that Candace's eyes are the same shape as my eyes, that they hadn't seen me awake. Bruce protested, "She looks like her momma." The label Down syndrome—I rolled it over in my mind, refusing to let it sink in. If it sinks in and I own it, then it would be true. *Down syndrome? No. We're not claiming that.* God's gifts and blessings often don't come packaged how we think. But since He knows me best, His gifts are always intentional.

THREE

GIFT BAG

Psalm 127:3 (NLT)
*Children are a gift from the Lord; they are
a reward from him.*

Have you ever gotten excited about a gift because of the beautiful wrapping paper? Maybe you assume that the perfect gift is inside because of the sparkly, shiny packaging. Perhaps you find out later that the priceless treasure was in a small obscure box.

Grappling with Uncertainty

I had three days in the hospital to grapple, sit in quiet, and trust God with the care of my babies. Cherie was with family and Candace was across town in Children's Hospital. I felt bad. I was missing precious bonding moments with my baby. At the same time, I felt fear. I would ponder, *what if she does have Down syndrome?* Would my child be one that society marginalized, the outcast- different than society? I was powerless. I could not intervene, I could not visit, but I started to have a sense of peace. God truly shielded her health condition of Down syndrome from us the entire pregnancy. My doctor did not mention the words *Down Syndrome*. In retrospect, my amniotic fluids were low, and she was more active after I ate. I thought she was thriving. This was a contrast from Cherie, who made my belly feel like a party house because she was active all the time. The doctors were surprised about everything that was going on with Candace. I imagined what might it have been like if I had been awake and paralyzed from the waist down while overhearing that she might have Down syndrome? Looking back, I wonder if that is why I was put to sleep. Our doctor was caught off-guard. He later mentioned that had we known ahead of time; I would have delivered at a different hospital that has a direct corridor to Children's Hospital. That way, I would have been able to visit as much as I wanted.

I remember people calling the hospital to congratulate us on the new baby and to inquire about how she was doing. *What do I say?* I was in no mood to talk and try to explain anything. I didn't want any advice. I needed to sort out my own feelings, but I did have a few people that I was able to pour my heart out to. Bruce's attention was divided, worrying about both me and Candace. He would visit me first and then take breast milk and the small blanket that I slept with that had my mother's scent to Candace. He would call me as soon as he arrived there at the hospital to give me an update. I would ask, "Well, does she have Down Syndrome? What does the doctor say?" All he could say was, "She is beautiful. I don't see Down syndrome. She is beautiful to me."

Even in that, God has had to mold my heart and my mindset that wanted to view it as a scar. Society uses the word "defect." What do you do with products that are defected? You return them or throw them away. We also use the word "invalid." In other words, this person doesn't matter. I needed to look at it from God's truth and not let society or other people's perspectives write the narrative. Every time Bruce would call, I would ask if he heard anything from the doctors. What was the verdict? Still no definite answer yet. They were running tests and treating her respiratory hypertension.

I did not know what this journey would look like. What would people say? I prayed to the Lord *if she does have Down syndrome; don't let it be obvious because I don't want her to be made fun of.* Why was this sensitivity to me? One, from a mother's heart, we have a desire to protect and shield our children. I remember the children in special education, who rode the "short bus." They were disabled, being the butt of many jokes and I did not want that for her. Or the fact that people with disabilities were never really seen. I remember in high school they were separated from the rest of the students. Or, people sometimes make a thoughtless comment like "Stop acting retarded. You're such a retard," or jokes or mannerisms mocking the disabled. These events flooded my mind. The Lord started to show me things about my personality and sensitivity, and my desire to be a voice for the voiceless, vulnerable and oppressed. God created me with special compassion for the outcasts of society.

When I was alone and especially at night, I would wrestle with God. God reminded me of the desires of my heart that I never could explain why I had them. At the time, they just seemed so random, but if she does have Down syndrome, it almost makes *more* sense. My desire for Cherie was to learn sign language. I wanted her to have friends with special needs. I wanted her to know that there are other people in the world who are different from her. I had a desire for a big house with wide hallways so that if someone came to visit that used a wheelchair, they would feel comfortable. I've always wanted to help shape policies that impact families and have always had a desire to live out my faith. Bruce and I would talk every night, and during this time, he was reminded of how he volunteered with the Special Olympics. Maybe God was preparing our hearts all along and knew the whole time. I thought back to how Bruce and I met while working in social service and how we shared a kindred spirit of helping vulnerable people. I remember Bruce would spend time with his neighbor, a high school student with an intellectual disability, just being his friend and teaching him life skills.

While in the hospital, I called some of my friends and they told me not to claim Down syndrome. That it is not God's will for her to have that. My prayer partner at the time, Joy, prayed with me and reminded me that God cares for Candace and holds her breath in His hands. She is made in the Image of God as it says in Genesis 1:27, "So God created mankind in his own image, in the image of God he created them; male and female he created them." I had heard that verse before but, when faced with the reality of potentially having a child with a disability; it took on a different meaning. I love that verse because it doesn't have caveats such as, "You're made in the image of God only *if* you are able-bodied," Or "You are made in the image of God, *except* individuals with Down syndrome or disabilities." So where do these caveats come from? Where does the stigma originate from? Because, to me, it didn't originate with God's purpose or plans for life.

When people started finding out about Candace and her condition, they had all different kinds of responses. I think most people do not know how to respond. In the beginning, one of the most memorable experiences for me was a friend from church who came to visit. I was able to pour my heart out to her. I shared my concerns and how the doctors think that Candace might have Down syndrome. She just sat quietly and listened. When I finished, she asked "Have you heard of Erma Brombeck? She wrote a poem a while ago about how God chooses special parents. I'll have to get you a copy." Her response was different and caught me off guard. *What was she saying but not saying?* Later, after it was all said and done, she told me that God had shown her our situation already. She knew in her heart that once I got over the initial shock, worked through my emotions and finally accepted it, I would be set free. I would realize that having a child with special needs was a desire of my heart, I just didn't know it yet.

Another response that impacted me deeply was the comment of a friend. She had a different reaction. She asked, "Why would God do that to

you? You are such a nice Christian lady!" I felt as
though she spoke for many in society. So many
people have this underlying belief that this is a
punishment because *I* have messed up some sort of
way. The devil has had a field day in this area. We
believe the lies that certain people have more
validity than others, but God in His word says that
He is no respecter of persons. Every child of God is
deeply loved and cherished by him with great
purpose.

The Longest Drive

I was finally released from the hospital to go and see
my baby. I was both excited and nervous. I was
overwhelmed with emotions and could not stop
crying all the way from the women's hospital to the
children's hospital. I went into the hospital to have a
baby and left empty-handed. There is something
wrong and unnatural about this situation. This
should not be. I knew that she was in safe hands, but
I'm her mother. I'm *supposed* to be there. Although I
knew I was going to see her, I kept looking at my

empty lap and empty car seat. I left the hospital with my overnight bag and nothing but discharge papers to document my visit. As I cried from Baptist West Hospital to Children's Hospital, there wasn't anything my husband could say to stop the tears. He just drove and gave me space to grieve. Oftentimes, we think of grief in the context of the death of a loved one, and rightfully so. My grief was in the loss of an expectation of a 'perfect' pregnancy, the loss of not being able to mother my child and the visualization of not carrying her home with me. With Cherie, Bruce had put the car seat in the car and the nurses had lined the hallway congratulating us while I held her in my lap while being wheeled to the front door in a wheelchair. Candace did not have that experience. We did not get to go straight home. There were no "Congratulations" or "It's a girl" balloons on our front door to welcome us home. We were not going home. Candace was not home. I grieved my expectations. I even grieved in dread of what if she does not make it?

I empathize with the mother who knows this experience all too well, whether through miscarriage or a stillborn. There is something unnatural about losing a child. It makes you feel cheated in some way and wrestle with questions of *Why me?* For parents who have experienced these tragedies, may you experience God's comfort in a supernatural way.

Bedside Manner

When I arrived at Children's Hospital, I was wheeled to the Neonatal Intensive Care Unit (NICU). I couldn't wait to hold Candace, but my attention was quickly drawn to the beautiful gift bag sitting next to her incubator. It was a gift bag from the Down Syndrome Awareness Group. Inside the bag were a down comforter and other resources. I would later find out that one of the nurses on the unit had a daughter with Down syndrome and had reached out to the Down Syndrome Awareness Groups (DSAG) community in advance on my behalf. In my heart, I continued to hold out for hope, while waiting on the "official" word, but I kept thinking about the stirring of my heart over the past three days. If she did have Down syndrome, it was still in the hands of God. But it wasn't official. Maybe the doctor would say something different or maybe she would have it but not with all the features. Maybe she'll outgrow it. Maybe we could get a second opinion. God can *still* work miracles.

While looking at Candace in her crib and waiting for the chance to hold her, the doctor walked in. He picked up her chart, and said, "Well," I responded, "Give me a minute." He replied, "If that is your response, then you know what it is. She has Down Syndrome." My heart dropped, it was official, final and permanent. She will not outgrow Down syndrome. She will experience the rest of her life through the framework of Down syndrome. Would that be all that society would see: Down syndrome? We grieved for our daughter. *What will she have to endure because she is different?* The deck was stacked against her.

Bruce and I wanted to protect her and shield her from the ugliness in the world. I was sad about the diagnosis but angry with the doctor. I felt that he was rude and insensitive. Not all doctors are this way, but when a doctor delivers the news every day, they can detach from people and just see problems and diagnoses. While he was talking, I noticed a nurse that was in perfect eyeshot and she was mouthing to me, "You're so blessed to have her." I was crying and Bruce was crying so we were taken into the next room, but that nurse just lingered as I was wheeled by. In the face of a difficult situation, she was there to speak life and words of encouragement. I wish that I could recall that nurse's name. It was providential that she was at the right place at the right time, speaking the truth and a higher perspective when our feelings were so low. It is in those low moments that we are often tempted to believe lies about our situation.

Bruce and I just cried and talked. I asked, "What does all of this mean?" At first, Bruce said nothing. Then, "I don't care what she has. I love Candace." That refreshed my heart and started to put things into perspective. Bruce was so supportive through everything. When crisis strikes, it's easy to play the blame game, but I thank God that we did not blame each other for a situation that was out of our control. Bruce was a rock for me and at the same time my soft place to land. His love for Candace was unconditional. He loved his daughter—all of her, with full and complete abandon. I carried Candace for nine months, but her earliest bonding moments were with her father. I know that he had his moments of fear and sadness, seeing his little baby in an incubator and on monitors. Bruce was the one that went to the NICU every day to spend time with Candace, tell her that it will be alright, make sure she knew that she was loved, and give her comfort. God designed marriage to be a partnership: when one person is weak, the other is strong. I was able to hold Candace for the first time and she was still as beautiful as I remember. I felt like she knew me because she just melted right into my arms. We had each other and it was going to be okay.

I had so many questions and very few answers. *What would it be like for BJ and Cherie having a sibling with special needs? What will their relationship be like?* Because Cherie and Candace were closer in age, I wondered if they would be teased at school. *What will Candace think about herself?* I asked BJ who was in high school what he observed in school about students with disabilities. His experience in school encouraged me. He talked about peer buddy programs where a non-disabled student is a peer/mentor for students with disabilities. Kids with disabilities were mainstreamed and included in school activities. BJ was always mature beyond his years and had a drive. He was a leader and always did very well in school, performing at the top of his class. When he found out that he would have a sister with Down syndrome, he recalls, "I just wanted her to know that she was loved. That was my main thing. I remember when I was in elementary school and some of the kids with Down syndrome would get picked on--I didn't like it." But that put a drive in him to be a peer tutor in high school for kids with disabilities. He spent time playing in the gym, teaching life skills, and being a friend. Society was changing for the better, which warmed this worried mother's heart, but we still have a long way to go. This generation of students is exposed to children with disabilities daily. In many cases, children with disabilities are no longer separated and school administrations and teachers are intentional about being inclusive. Awareness of disability is increasing through education, commercials, and "people- first" language. We still have a long way to go to break off stereotypes and change perceptions of our society about individuals with a disability, but this kind of change takes time, and we will get there little by little.

FOUR

FRAGILE: HANDLE WITH CARE

Jeremiah 29:11
*For I know the plans I have for you,"
declares the Lord, "plans to prosper you
and not to harm you, plans to give you a
hope and a future.*

Have you ever received a gift that you would not have asked for, only later to find out it's what you needed all along? Was it a gift you would come to appreciate later in life? Around the time I was 7 years old, my grandmother gave me a child-sized china tea set. It was beautiful, even though I couldn't play with it like I could with the rest of my toys and dolls because it was delicate and fragile. It was not for everyday use. My grandmother set it in her china cabinet with her expensive dishes that we only used for company and on holidays. I could use it under adult supervision and for special occasions. I appreciate the memory of that gift so much now because it taught me about real value and worth. I gained a deeper understanding of my own value and worth too, that I could be trusted with such a precious gift at such a young age. My grandmother knew me better than I knew myself. God is the same way; He knows us better than we know ourselves.

Down syndrome

We met with Candace's geneticist to confirm the diagnosis and she showed us Candace's chromosomes. I thought maybe we would get a second opinion to which she responded as far as chromosomes; the science is there. "If you had known when you were pregnant, you could have done something different, but, oh well. She's here now. If you had her 30 years ago, I would have recommended you put her in an institution. Nowadays, they do alright in a good home, but she will not be a doctor or lawyer." Maybe the mindset 30 years ago was that individuals with Down syndrome could not contribute to society. Or perhaps, why spend resources on individuals who won't amount to much? Maybe we're better off if they are not here. The weight of her words struck me because she was a professional. Her words carried authority to influence and chart the trajectory of a person's life. Instead of offering hope to us overwhelmed and fearful parents, we left feeling more discouraged. We took it upon ourselves to learn about Down syndrome. We would mold and shape of Candace's life. We will be her biggest fans and the words we speak over her will give life and hope.

Down syndrome, Trisomy 21, is three copies of the 21st Chromosome. The odds of having a child with Down syndrome are 1/1000. For me, the odds were 1/932. According to the Centers for Disease Control, "Down syndrome is a condition in which a person has an extra chromosome. Chromosomes are small packages of genes in our body. They determine how a baby forms and grows outside the body. People with Down Syndrome usually have an IQ in the mildly-to-moderately low-range, are slower to speak than other children." This is all in addition to increased health problems such as hearing loss, heart defects, eye diseases, ear infections, and obstructive sleep apnea. Individuals also have common physical features: flattened face, a short neck, almond-shaped eyes, a tongue thrust that tends to stick out of the mouth, small hands and feet, palms crease, small pinky fingers, poor muscle tone or loose joints, shorter in height as children and adults. (cdc.gov)

I did not present any risks of having a child with Down syndrome, so I had no reason to be concerned or even consider it. One risk that is often cited for being a cause for Down Syndrome is the age of the mother being over 35, which was not the case for us because I was 31 at the time of having Candace. I do not claim to know all the plans and purposes of God, but I have come to realize that he knows me better than I know myself. I wondered why God did not give me a heads up but, then again, He does not have to run anything past me or ask my permission. I thought about the geneticist's comment, "You could have done something different had you found out while you were pregnant." When the doctor listed all that Candace would not be, I praise God that I had a firm foundation to keep me grounded. I believe life begins at the moment of conception and Candace is made with intrinsic value and worth. What I knew then and I know now, is that Candace will be all that

God created her to be. The geneticist did not leave me hopeful, so I had to rely on God's word. God formed Candace perfectly and by what may be called a fluke, He knit her together with His hands.

Feeling Inadequate

While at the hospital, Candace thrived very well. We experienced answered prayer along the way. She did not have any feeding issues and was able to latch on and be breastfed. Candace passed both her hearing and vision screenings, and her oxygen levels had increased. It is not uncommon for children with Down Syndrome to have heart issues. She did have separations in her heart but nothing that needed correcting at the time. In fact, the doctor expected the separations to close on their own over time. We praised God because Candace was already proving how she was a fighter.

One afternoon while still at the hospital I was holding and rocking Candace, talking to her and just spending time with her. The Social Worker approached and sat with us and eased into a tough conversation. She started talking about the benefits that might be available for children with special health needs, such as Social Security, early intervention services, support groups, and special education. It dawned on me to ask, "You're saying my daughter is disabled?" I guess I knew it but hadn't realized what all Down syndrome entailed. This gradual loss, it put us in another category: our baby is disabled.

I had worked in social services as a case manager and in other aspects but experiencing the gentleness and compassion of our medical social worker spurred a desire in me to become a Social Worker. Social Work is a protected profession with educational and licensing requirements and a Code of Ethics. In those moments, talking to her, I thought, *I want to do that:* be trained and equipped to walk alongside parents and families in tough situations. I want to be that voice that says, "It is going to be ok." I want to bring peace in the midst of a storm. At that moment, I had a glimpse of myself further along on this path and reaching back lifting up another parent. Because of our shared journey, I would be able to handle broken parents softly as our social worker did with us.

Candace spent a total of 11 days in the NICU. When it was time for me to take her home, I remember lingering and staying as long as I possibly could, because I knew that when I left that hospital we would be on our own and I felt inadequate. The nurses at the hospital were professionals and had been in situations like this. They knew what to do. They would make the right decisions. They had training in this, but we did not. This was uncharted territory. How exactly do you care for a child with Down Syndrome? Candace was fragile. We had to handle her with special care. I did not want to mess up or do anything wrong. The hospital had already scheduled upcoming appointments to see specialists and follow up with her pediatrician, but that all felt overwhelming to me. How can I keep track of all these dates? I also felt a spirit of fear grip me. Candace had been thriving and receiving promising reports, but with all the appointments looming ahead I felt on edge, anticipating the worst. *What's going to happen next? What will the doctor say?* Fortunately, the nurse caught on to my stalling tactics and had to give me a stern reality check. She said, "This is your baby, first. Down syndrome is secondary. She will cry and need feeding; she will need to be held and loved. If you are doing that, everything will take care of itself. Get a calendar and handle one day at a time. Trust your instinct and you will make the right decisions for her." Her encouraging words grounded me. Because truthfully, Candace was okay, I was okay, our family was okay, and we were all going to be okay. I will not always get the answers right, but I must believe what is true. *"Whatever is true, whatever is noble, whatever is right, whatever is pure, whatever is lovely, whatever is admirable - if anything is excellent or praiseworthy- think about such things."* Philippians 4:8

This perspective allowed me to focus on bonding with my baby, being present in the moment and loving Candace without reservations. 1 John 4:18, *"There is no fear in love. But perfect love drives out fear."* I cannot fully love her if my heart is gripped with all kinds of fear: fear of tomorrow, negative doctor reports, making a mistake and most seriously, of her dying. I had to make a choice to believe that God chose me to be her mother and whatever decision I make as a mother was from a place of love and in Candace's best interest. This is a choice I have every day. I choose to love at this moment.

FIVE

RE-PURPOSED GIFTS

2 Corinthians 12:9
"But he said to me, 'My grace is sufficient for you, for my power is made perfect in weakness.' Therefore, I will boast all the more gladly about my weaknesses, so that Christ's power may rest on me."

Going through this process challenged me to be more authentic and genuine in my relationships with others, with God, and with myself. My personality is to want to help *others,* so having a need myself made me feel vulnerable. I like being of use to others and I dislike needing help from them. But

I am not all-sufficient; I need the help and support of others. My life would forever be changed through this experience, challenging me to be more transparent and to gain deeper compassion for others. I also learned about humility and weakness. I was on equal footing with everyone else. I could no longer give a cliché response to others' sufferings like, "It's going to be alright," "Let me pray for you," or "God's got it." Now, I could provide a deeper level of empathy and understanding. I could relate to others in their pain and from personal experience be fully present without judging. Part of my evolution was first being honest with myself about how I was feeling—my concerns and fears.

More importantly, I had to be honest with God. I knew in my head and heart that I was blessed to have Candace, but I was uncertain about my feelings toward Down syndrome. I wanted my emotions to hurry up and catch up with my intellect. My emotions were inconsistent: I was happy for a new baby but sad at the same time. Two things were true for me simultaneously: I loved Candace--she is a blessing and I am grateful. But I was also afraid and sad when I thought about what life was going to be like for her. I had walked with the Lord long enough to know that Candace having Down syndrome was not random, nor was He caught off guard. He was not wringing his hands saying, "I did not see *that* coming! What am I going to do now?" I believe that He was up to something bigger than what I could see. He had a greater purpose and an eternal plan. He always does. I do not believe in coincidence, but instead, my steps are purposed and planned. I knew the Lord was going to help me reconcile my vacillating mind. James 1:4-6 and 8, *"Let perseverance finish its work so that you may be mature and complete, not lacking anything. If any of*

you lacks wisdom, you should ask God, who gives
generously to all without finding fault and it will be
given to you. But when you ask, you must believe
and not doubt, because the one who doubts is like a
wave of the sea, blown and tossed by the wind...
Such a person is double-minded and unstable in all
they do."

What I knew for sure was that I did not want
to be a phony. Have you ever met someone and you
asked genuinely, "How are you?" and they respond
with, "I'm blessed!" or "Girl, God is good all the
time." For me, I want to be sincere when I say it, not
flippantly saying it because it is the nice 'Christian'
thing. I desire to be *real*. If it hurts, I want to say
that. Or, "God, this is not making sense to me."
Some people live their lives believing that they
should not ask God questions. I believe God wants
us to ask Him all of our hard questions because He
desires intimacy with us. The truth is, God is a big
God and can handle our tough questions. In fact,
vulnerability is attractive to Him. Once I opened

myself up and started to engage in a conversation, God responded.

Through all of my questions, He reminded me of some women I knew and their journeys with this wrestling. God showed me how they handled tough situations and the miracles He worked in their lives. Not all of these women had raised children with disabilities, but they all had a crisis of faith situation that required them to trust God's character in the face of tough circumstances. I remembered a dear mentor of mine battling breast cancer and she stayed strong and resilient against the odds. I think of my mother, who was a teenager when she had me, later coming to know the Lord and choosing to raise me in a Christian home even though the deck was stacked against us. She chose to teach a godly standard and not lean on her own understanding or upbringing to set the tone for how she lived or how she raised me. The standard was a biblical view of morality, marriage and raising kids.

We had a generational history of teen parents, drinking alcohol, and getting high but she had faith to know that she wanted better and more for me, despite our family history and the culture around us. I would be the first generation that would live differently. I then think of my grandmother, choosing to open her home to start Bible Studies for single moms and teach inner-city kids with the little she had. My grandmother would volunteer at a Christian school to offset the cost of my tuition so that I could have quality education and change the trajectory of our family's course. These stories would help to shoulder and support me when I needed it. I may not have understood all the details then, but on this journey of womanhood, and now motherhood, we are all connected. We all share love and concern of our children being vulnerable, harmed, bullied, or teased. *Who will nurture them? What if I am not here? Are they safe? Will they be protected?* When we pull the layers off, race, economic status, and location do not matter. We *all* cry and feel pain.

Now that I'm older, I can relate. I too am in that shared space. I was pregnant during the 2008 historic presidential election and regardless of the outcome, this country was going to be in a place that it had never been before. Whether it was the election of the first African- American President or electing a woman as Vice-President, something that stood out to me was how Sarah Palin would talk about her son, Trigg. I remember wondering what it was like to raise a child with Down syndrome. She must be a strong lady. She takes him everywhere with her. The whole family seems to love and support him. Unbeknownst to me, I was carrying a child with Down syndrome. Maybe that was God's way to help warm me up to the idea, but also give me a frame of reference that did not have a stigma or shame attached to it. He showed me a family that was further along on the journey so I could see that life still goes on. Our God is so specifically good like that.

I appreciated everyone else's testimony and the way that God used other struggles to remind me of his faithfulness. We need to remember all that God has done in each other's lives. It encourages us and builds us up. Maybe that is why the Israelites were called to remember so often in the Old Testament (see Joshua 4:7). Now, it was my turn. In this situation, I needed my own testimony. After we brought Candace home and were trying to get settled in, Bruce returned to work, and it was just me and Candace at home. I remember praying, *God, you must speak to me. I don't want to go through life giving lip service. When I say, 'I'm blessed.' I want to mean it, and the only way for that to happen is for you to speak to me. Speak to my*

> **Luke 1:26-45**
> 26 In the sixth month of Elizabeth's pregnancy, God sent the angel Gabriel to Nazareth, a town in Galilee, 27 to a virgin pledged to be married to a man named Joseph, a descendant of David. The virgin's name was Mary. 28 The angel went to her and said, "Greetings, you who are highly favored! The Lord is with you." 29 Mary was greatly troubled at his words and wondered what kind of greeting this might be. 30 But the angel said to her, "Do not be afraid, Mary; you have found favor with God. 31 You will conceive and give birth to a son, and you are to call him Jesus.

heart. I specifically asked the Lord to speak to me directly- what I knew in my head I needed to internalize it and be inspired in my heart. In my head, I knew that Candace was a blessing. However, my feelings needed to catch up. God was about to answer that prayer.

Most days of the week, I would have a quiet time which usually consisted of Scripture reading and prayer. This evening was no different. I am not sure how I ended up in the following passage of scripture, but it was the Rhema-right now word that I needed.

32 He will be great and will be called the Son of the Most High. The Lord God will give him the throne of his father David, 33 and he will reign over Jacob's descendants forever; his kingdom will never end." 34 "How will this be," Mary asked the angel, "since I am a virgin?" 35 The angel answered, "The Holy Spirit will come on you, and the power of the Most High will overshadow you. So the holy one to be born will be called the Son of God. 36 Even Elizabeth your relative is going to have a child in her old age, and she who was said to be unable to conceive is in her sixth month. 37 For no word from God will ever fail." 38 "I am the Lord's servant," Mary answered. "May your word to me be fulfilled." Then the angel left her. 39 At that time Mary got ready and hurried to a town in the hill country of Judea, 40 where she entered Zechariah's home and greeted Elizabeth. 41 When Elizabeth heard Mary's greeting, the baby leaped in her womb, and Elizabeth was filled with the Holy Spirit. 42 In a loud voice she exclaimed: "Blessed are you among women, and blessed is the child you will bear! 43 But why am I so favored, that the mother of my Lord should come to me? 44 As soon as the sound of your greeting reached my ears, the baby in my womb leaped for joy. 45 Blessed is she who has believed that the Lord would fulfill his promises to her!"

For the first time, I got it. I have read this passage numerous times and have heard the Christmas Story, but today was different. This passage stood up off the page and jumped in my heart. It was a fresh revelation. I understood what it was like to be a woman who was different; to have something imposed on you that you did not ask for. Besides, who is going to believe that Mary was a virgin? "She treasured these things in her heart." Surely Mary was like other mothers who are concerned about people teasing her child. Not only was she different, but so was her child. She lived in a community just like I do. People talk and gossip. After I read the passage, the Holy Spirit impressed on my heart, *go back and read it again, but put* your *name in there*:

> "Meka do not be afraid. The Lord is with you; you are blessed, and you have favor."

His presence is with me. He was not asleep in heaven, letting my family slip through the cracks. His presence, power, and peace are with me. I have been looking at this all wrong. God could have placed Candace in any family he chose to. Instead, look what He thought about *me*. Look what He thought of *Bruce*. Look what He thought about my family. This is not a fluke. God's perspective brought peace and healing. I felt more empowered, and honestly more alive, like every desire of my heart was leading up to this moment. God was not caught off guard, and his providential hand was orchestrating our life's events and desires to bring me to this point. I noted Mary's response: "I am your servant, at your word, Lord." I chose to echo the same sentiment.

I remember telling Bruce what I had read because I had found a new joy and freedom. God put it in my heart: *I want to help other people.*

SIX

GREAT TREASURE— UNIQUE PACKAGES

Romans 8:26-28

In the same way, the Spirit helps us in our weakness. We do not know what we ought to pray for, but the Spirit himself intercedes for us through wordless groans. And he who searches our hearts knows the mind of the Spirit, because the Spirit intercedes for God's people in accordance with the will of God. And we know that in all things God works for the good of those who love him, who have been called according to his purpose.

Sometimes we do not realize what we need in life until after we have received it. We think we know what we want and often, our prayers are from a place of *our* understanding, birthed out of our fears or desire for answers that will help make our life more convenient. Do we truly pray the heart of God and the will of God for our lives? I'll be the first to admit, I have often approached prayer with a solution in mind before I present God with the problem. Basically, I want Him to co-sign on what I think is in my own best interest, when I have a limited perspective on my situation.

The above-referenced verse helps to drive this home. The Holy Spirit is the spirit of God and goes in between, buffering and adjusting my prayers so that the outcome is in alignment with God's perfect will for me. I think intercession is two-fold: The Holy Spirit is praying to the Father on my behalf, and at the same time preparing my heart, renewing my mind and tweaking my desires so that they agree and are ready for the answer. My desires need to be tweaked because the answer oftentimes does not show up how we think it should. If we were shown the big picture, all that life had in store, we would either run from or pick and choose our experiences. Walking by faith is just that: not having all the answers or knowing the outcomes. Rather, it is trusting that the disappointment and heartache will balance out with the achievements and joyful times. And that, in the end, it all will work together in the greater scheme of life for good.

This is how I envision my prayer exchange with the Lord: "Lord, I pray for a baby boy. That would be perfect! A picture-perfect family." Holy Spirit then mediates and cleans it up, "What she is trying to say is, she wants your perfect will in this. She is submitted to you. Your will is to do exceedingly abundantly more than she can ask, think, or imagine (Ephesians 3:20). Answer her prayer by giving her the *real* desires of her heart. Desires that you, Father, placed there. Your heart for the vulnerable and oppressed. Your heart for the disabled. This family will be your voice. Having a child with special needs will teach them to see others the way You see them. They will be advocates—your advocates. These are their true desires." The Holy Spirit then searches my heart, the depths of me, and draws out hopes that I am not fully aware of and presents those petitions to Father God.

Is this not the center of the Gospel of Jesus Christ? Humankind has limitations and imperfections, for we all have sinned and fall short of God's glory (Romans 3:23). Jesus became our advocate, our mediator because we were helpless and could not save ourselves. He showed us mercy and offered us forgiveness. Micah 7:18, "Who is a God like you, who pardons sin and forgives the transgression of the remnant of his inheritance? You do not stay angry forever but delight to show mercy."

God was not trying to take something away from me. He was trying to give some things to me: the abundant life, His promises, and walking in the purposes and calling for our life, our marriage, and our family. He was calling me higher, to be all that He has created me to be. He did give me the desires of my heart. When I think of those seemingly random inklings or desires, this was all part of his master plan.

Our New Normal

We did not have a clue what to expect on our new journey into the world of special health needs. Children with special needs require more care for their physical, developmental, behavioral, or emotional differences than their typically developing peers (Centers for Disease Control, 2018). We had a primary care physician that we heard wonderful things about and his expertise in treating pediatrics with Down syndrome. He was encouraging and knowledgeable. I could tell that he had guided new parents down this road of uncertainty before. The main thing was that I always left his practice feeling hopeful.

We attempted to enroll Candace in Gerber Life Insurance, but she was turned down. They said to call back in five years. We felt slighted because we saw our baby, but the insurance company saw a liability and that hurt. This is the tension we would continue to live in, these two opposing viewpoints: our view as parents and wanting what is best versus the professionals who, at times, only viewed Candace through charts and graphs—not seeing what we see. In our conversations, we would voice our frustrations because we felt powerless. For me, this frustration turned to prayers and just sad moments. For Bruce, it created a drive and sustained his commitment to take care of us.

We enrolled Candace in early intervention right away. "Early intervention is a voluntary educational program for families with children birth through age two with disabilities or developmental delays." (Tennessee Early Intervention System-tn.gov). I personally think that her best therapist has been her older sister. Cherie just saw a little sister to play with and love on. She made sure that Candace played. Candace would do her best to keep up. Even though I had God's word which blessed me, changed my perspective, and gave me hope, I still felt isolated at times because no other parent was going through what I was going through. There were things in my heart that I did not feel like I could talk about to anyone, only lift them up in prayer. I learned to depend on God in new and deeper ways. When I would read the Bible, I saw the sensitivity that God has for the vulnerable. (see Leviticus 19:14)

I started to look at life through the lens of disability because it affected our lives. When a friend would call, it was like they did not know what questions to ask. It was general topics like, "How are the girls?" I replied, "Oh, they are good." Who really knew what I was feeling or what I was afraid of? During this time, I was a stay at home mom. I felt like Bruce had an outlet because he could go to work, have an adult conversation, and leave parenting at the house. I had to handle the day-to-day, not just diapering, but my concerns about tomorrow. I felt like there was so much uncertainty. Parents in general, you know that seasons will change. So yes, you might be frustrated and over changing diapers but give it a couple of years, and that season will be over. I knew I would not be changing diapers forever, but when that season ends- who knows what comes next?

As Candace developed, we used some Down Syndrome growth charts as a guide. She was off the charts in height and weight but had delays in other areas of development. I felt that was God's way of saying even in this she is still unique and cannot fit into a mold. We will not compare. We would celebrate Candace's progress and learn from others' experience while keeping everything in perspective. Both of our children have special needs and are individuals. Train them up because they have a natural bent and propensity (Proverb 22:6).

Candace's schedule also required therapy three times a week: speech, physical and occupational therapy. The physical therapy addressed gross motor skills, rolling over, sitting up, head control, crawling and walking. Occupational therapy dealt with fine motor skills, grasping, holding objects and blocks. Speech therapy worked with Candace on feeding, such as making sounds and feeding using a sippy cup and eating finger foods. Our life revolved around therapy appointments, and I needed something for Cherie. We did not plan on a pre-school program for her, but I was at a women's function and a friend, who was there, mentioned a school in the heart of Knoxville that was enrolling new students. Cherie was three years old at the time. We went to visit the school and what impressed me most was the intentional pairing of a preschool student with a foster grandparent. Not only was Cherie receiving a quality pre-school education, but she was also an outlet for the grandparents. This was a place that instilled character, values and a love for learning. Preschool was also a place of encouragement for me. I think of the times the mature women would give me advice about parenting and being a wife. I gleaned so much from their life experience. The grandmothers would say, "Don't worry, she gon' get it. She gon' be alright." I researched the impact of having a sibling with special needs, and honestly, she was light years ahead of me. I asked her how she was doing and what she thought about Candace's disability. I was expecting a deep, profound answer, but what I got was, "I don't think about Down syndrome. It's just Candace."

I retained the sign language videos that I had used with Cherie and taught Candace basic sign language to encourage communication. Early Intervention would send out an educator once or twice a week to our home and provide tips to work with Candace and ways we could modify our house without breaking the bank. They also gave us home exercises to do with Candace. We practiced strengthening activities to encourage sitting, crawling, standing and later walking. She developed reaching and grasping objects. This was our daily routine for the first three years.

Cherie was very in-tune with what was going on. I remember one-time Cherie had a friend over to watch a movie and the little girl asked if we could turn up the volume. Cherie, in all sincerity, asked, "Do you need ear tubes?" I laughed, but this is our normal. Cherie had to mature quicker than the other three, four or five-year-olds, but that exposure was good. She asked this because, at this point, Candace had her first set of ear tubes placed. She was around 16 months. This procedure required an overnight stay in the hospital. What made us, as parents, very nervous, was the use of anesthesia and her having to be put to sleep. Candace was retaining fluid in her ears and placing ear tubes would help with the drainage. In turn, enabling her to hear clearly. In Cherie's mind, this was a natural remedy for any hearing and volume issues. Bless her heart! Overhearing her response made me feel that including friends with disabilities would not be unusual for her. Moreover, she would have empathy for those who look or act differently. She was learning to not be judgmental and to be accepting of others. This warmed my mother's heart.

SEVEN

THE BIRTH OF A MINISTRY

2 Corinthians 1:3-5
Praise be to the God and Father of our Lord Jesus Christ, the Father of compassion and the God of all comfort, who comforts us in all our troubles, so that we can comfort those in any trouble with the comfort we ourselves receive from God. For just as we share abundantly in the sufferings of Christ, so also our comfort abounds through Christ.

Down Syndrome Awareness Group of East Tennessee (DSAG) was a great support for us. We met other families that experienced a similar situation. We attended the Christmas Parties, Zoo outings, Dollywood, and exchanged phone numbers to keep in touch. DSAG families became an extended family to us. One thing I appreciated most was the fact that there was "No shame." I felt like we could have honest conversations. Parents raising a child with special health needs have a kindred spirit. Oftentimes when meeting a new person, we tend to stay guarded and only disclose information on an as-needed basis, because you don't know that person. Conversations tend to be shallow, talking the weather or other surface issues. In comparison, when meeting a fellow parent with a child with a disability, their life is already on display. Meaning, you know that they have cried, experienced heartache, fear and felt vulnerable. You know, that they have laughed hard because they have learned to appreciate the simple things other parents might take for granted. They know all too well about miracles because they have seen their child do what others thought couldn't be done. I was blessed by the parents that were further along on the journey, they instilled hope.

We participated in our first Buddy Walk. Buddy Walk that promotes inclusion and raises awareness of individuals with Down syndrome (National Down Syndrome Society). All I could do was cry. Our family created posters for Candace to include pictures of her and Cherie and our normal daily life. It was surreal to see all the other families gathered in one place to celebrate Down syndrome. We were more alike than different. Parents, advocates, teachers and all who cared about someone with Down Syndrome was there to show support, change the narrative and perspective about individuals with Down Syndrome. I reflected on the comment that if I had her 30 years ago she could have been institutionalized. Today, society is changing. Down Syndrome is not a scar but a gift to the world.

As we became more involved with our local awareness group, I started to wonder what supports were available in minority communities. Were minorities accessing the services they needed? On a broader note, how does culture impact the way we view a person with a disability? Education is key. I enjoy studying research. Owning to, my roles as a wife, mother and social worker, I have a natural curiosity about family- dynamics, specifically, families affected by disability.

God used my background to birth a vision in me to see families encouraged about having a child with a disability from a Christ-centered perspective. Perhaps I should start a non-profit. But where do I start? I don't even have a name. One day, I was listening to the radio and Chuck Swindoll delivered a message "When God's gifts come specially wrapped." That's It! That's the name "Specially Wrapped Gifts." Specially Wrapped Gifts, because children are a gift from God and ours came specially wrapped. This outreach would address heart and spirit issues along with the practical needs of families. Resources are wonderful and needed, but if you go through life without a foundational perspective of God's vision for your child and situation, then these resources have only addressed one part of the issue. Society has placed value on things like appearance, wealth, and success, so it is easy to think that is what is valuable to God. We project our worldviews onto God instead of His view shaping our view of the world. What does it mean to be made in the image of God? There are no caveats or exceptions to the rule. Our value is inherent. Our purpose comes from our identity in Christ, not on how we look or what our abilities are. We wanted to bring hope from a truth perspective to families like ours. That is the vision of this non-profit. Our mission is, "To demonstrate the love of Christ to families affected by special health needs and/or disability by providing encouragement and resources."

The Scripture above is one that I have grown to treasure. There are just so many truths you can collect from it. It reminds me that God is the source for all comfort, and He promises that my heartache or pain will not be wasted. Instead, I am to use my experience to identify with someone else who is hurting and strengthen them in their trial. God has a myriad of ways that He can bring us comfort: by leading us to read-a specific verse or passage or by connecting us with other people to encourage one another.

An Advocate for Both

After some research, I found that supports are there for the person with the disability, but they are limited when addressing the family. The reality is, if a child has special health needs, the entire family is impacted. For example, mom and dad have the task of being a perpetual parent with extended caregiving and the increased strain in their marriage. We had to be intentional in our marriage to keep it first and that takes work. Secondly, siblings are deeply impacted when they have a brother or sister with a disability. We knew that Cherie having a sister with Down Syndrome was unique, an experience that most peers her age would not be able to relate to. According to Conway and Meyer (2008), "1 in 10 children have special health, developmental and mental health concerns; most have non-disabled siblings."

We looked for enrichment activities for Cherie and learned about Sibshops: Workshops for Siblings of Children with Special Needs (2009). She was too young to attend our local group, but I latched on to the concept of ensuring that she had the support she needed to address her needs. I wanted to make sure she had peer relationships with siblings of individuals affected by special health needs and age-appropriate education about Candace's diagnosis. The relationship between siblings typically lasts longer than any other relationship, even after the parents have died. Siblings often share the same experiences that their siblings face such as isolation, in addition to concerns about the future and feelings of guilt (Conway and Meyer 2008 & Rawson 2009).

We took a less structured approach in addressing our concern for Cherie to feel supported. We established an open line of communication with her schoolteachers. Additionally, we fostered relationships with families in our Down syndrome awareness group and Cherie was able to form lasting friendships there with siblings around her age. She was encouraged to ask us questions, and we had great physical, speech and occupational therapists that answered her questions and looked for ways to make therapy fun so that Cherie could play games with her sister at home.

It is a balancing act. In the disability community "special needs" is thrown around a lot, when, all children have special needs. I am working on being more intentional to use the term "special health needs" instead. One day Cherie asked me if she was special. Her question bothered me. She internalized a message that she was a run of the mill and that was a lie. I explained to her that she is special! I affirmed who she is. Reminded her of why we chose to name her Cherie "Cherry." God made her unique- one of a kind. Beautiful with thick and full hair, dark complexion, high cheekbones, articulate, wise and witty. Compassionate with a love for justice. She brings joy to our family and she is a gift to the world. How proud I am to be her mother. I empathized with Cherie, stepped into her shoes and viewed life from her perspective. I understood how she could feel not special.

For our family, we wanted to be intentional that both Cherie and Candace feel special and not only relate to Cherie in relation to Candace. If you have a child with a disability, they require more attention: doctor's appointments, individualized educational goals and the milestones they make are celebrated because they can be fewer and farther between. There is more to Cherie than being Candace's sister. This is true for all siblings of children with special health needs. Yes, it is an aspect of her life, just as Down syndrome is an aspect of Candace's life, but neither role totally defines who they are. Labels are necessary for transmitting information quickly and for streamlining communication, but when they are used to pigeon-hole or perpetuate stereotypes, then labeling becomes a problem. I am not only an advocate for Candace to ensure that she receives the services, support, dignity, and inclusion that she needs. I am passionate about raising awareness about the utilization of people-first language. For example, what do you hear when someone says, "A Down's Child?" I hear limits, what they cannot do. How about the phrase "A child with Down Syndrome?" She is a person *first*. This small tweak in the way we communicate about people makes all the difference. We need to move past the convenience and put people first. She is a cheerleader on a special needs team, funny, creative, sensitive to other's needs, and she enjoys playing baby dolls. Oh, and she has Down Syndrome. I also find it important to be an advocate for Cherie as well. I recall an event that I enrolled both girls in and the director figured that they could place both together in the same class, that way Cherie could help with Candace if need be. Part of being Cherie's advocate means saying "No." Cherie needs space to work on her own activities.

Besides, that is what the staff of this event is for: to engage both individually. Both need space to grow, learn and develop their gifts.

Bruce and I are intentional and want to make sure that Cherie knows that she is loved, that she is special, and that she has the space to discover her gifts and qualities. One thing that I appreciate about Bruce is that he makes it a point to spend time with both girls but each of them has a special thing they do together. For Bruce and Cherie, both share a love of superheroes and movies. For Candace, on more than one occasion, I have caught him playing dolls with her. My prayer is that Cherie is affirmed, knows that she is loved, is seen and heard. She not only matters to God, but to us as well. It is important that we as the parents meet each child individually where they are. After all, that is what God does with us.

Addressing Spiritual Wounds

I found that with the abundance of resources for families experiencing disability, there was a lack of those that address the spiritual side of being affected with disability. I reflected on the comments that my friend made to me, that God was "punishing me", and sensed others in society probably share that same sentiment. There have been numerous occasions when I have shared about having a child with Down syndrome. The response is often, "I'm sorry." Sorry about what? We are not sorry, and in fact, are so blessed to have her! I personally could not imagine bearing the weight of thinking that God is mad at me, or that I am cursed and that he is exacting some sort of revenge on me. Some people in society might want me to believe that, but it is inconsistent with my understanding of God's character. As a matter of fact, when I read scriptures, I see God's compassion and sensitivity to the vulnerable and disabled. Here are a few lessons I have learned along this journey:

- I have learned to not be so quick to say that I know something that God has been silent about because I don't know all the plans of purposes of God (John 9:1-12).

- I have learned that God made us all both able-bodied and differently-abled (Exodus 4:11).

- I have learned that God is drawn to the vulnerable and receives glory out of using individuals that are marginalized or shunned to show His love to the world (1 Corinthians 1:27-28).

In addition to all the resources we could provide, we also wanted to get to the spiritual side of issues and approach them from a foundation of Truth. The Bible says we are all made in God's image with inherent value, dignity, and worth.

I am unsure how the idea came about, but one day, Bruce and I decided to have a luncheon in the inner city. Growing up in the inner city along with our social service experience, I knew this would be an area with great needs but limited resources. We wanted to meet parents in the local community and host a beautiful luncheon- free to them. We wanted to love on them, let them know they were not alone, and provide encouragement.

When I decided to plan the event, things started to fall in place. I reconnected with a good friend and she volunteered to make the programs while other people offered to help with the food. I had to take the walk of faith and God put the people in place to support the vision. We passed out fliers in the community and to local churches.

We made connections with some of the families there. Baby steps, right? Later that year, we hosted a picnic in the same area. One of the attendees was a grandmother raising her grandchildren. One of her grandsons was school-aged and going through chemotherapy. Having a child with special health needs can be isolating, so these events were a great way to connect with others. It was a place to network and start to erase the shame of a taboo subject.

Our Christian faith is the center of our family and shapes our beliefs, mindset, and worldview. From this foundation, the Church should be the most accepting. I started to feel somewhat frustrated because when I looked around and reflected over the years, I could not remember a time that individuals with disabilities were fully integrated or embraced as an active part of Church life. Yes, they were welcome, but churches were not proactive or intentional to make sure they felt included.

When Candace was about one, we were visiting a church and she was crying in the nursery. They paged us to come and get her. My husband went back to check on her, then later called me. When I spoke with the nursery staff, they told us that we should put her in the special needs Sunday school class, which consisted of much older children with autism. I was angry. She was not crying because she had Down syndrome, but because she was a baby and they cry. People in our society get hung up on the label and tend to lump "special needs" together. Relating this experience is not meant to disparage the Body of Christ. I think they were doing the best they knew to do, especially if they had not received any training on Down Syndrome or special health needs for that matter. I realize that most nursery workers in churches are volunteers who serve from the kindness of their heart, but how can we support and welcome families who are impacted by a disability? Do families feel accepted? Additionally, how can we better equip ministry volunteers? Since we are made in the image of God, church and faith communities should be the most accepting.

One Sunday, my sister invited me to the House of Worship Church in Oak Ridge, Tennessee. The usher that day was Keila, a young African American woman with Down syndrome. She was ushering at the door with her mother. Candace was about two or three at the time. When Candace saw Keila for the first time, she was mesmerized and stared like she was looking in a mirror. In my heart, I felt the Lord saying, "Meka, I got you. Candace is going to be alright." Our prayers continually have been that the girls would know the Lord personally and have their own relationship with Him. I wanted Candace to have her own walk with the Lord, learning to trust Him for herself and using her gifts in church and society. At that moment, everything I had prayed and the stirrings of my mother's heart, God answered. It was more than what the pastor preached that day; the church's acceptance and love spoke volumes to me.

It turned out that Keila's mom was a school occupational therapist who gave me practical tips on how to work with Candace. As our relationship grew, I was able to share my heart with her and she suggested that I talk to Pastor Collins about hosting an encouragement group at the church to provide practical advice from a Christ-centered perspective to families with children with disabilities.

This encouragement group began meeting once a month and we had volunteers from the church who watched the kids. It was a safe space for parents to share, pray, and not feel judged. I would come up with a topic of discussion or we would invite someone to speak to us. Topics included:

- Ways to prevent caregiver burnout

- How to prepare for Individual Educational Plan meetings

- Family dynamics

- Learning to trust God during tough times

One of our regular attendees, *Renee, was a single parent with five children. Her son had Down syndrome and other disabilities. I remember at one of our gatherings, she approached me and asked if we could include her other son because it was his birthday and she had not had the chance to get ice cream. So, we made it a celebration for him as well. Disability impacts the entire family and oftentimes parents are overwhelmed and burnt out with the day to day caregiving.

During the Christmas season, we would all get together and have a Christmas dinner. Local organizations donated gifts to Specially Wrapped Gifts families and our church family would serve the meal. I cherished those days because we could share our experience of raising a child with disabilities and be a shoulder for each other. Children with special health needs/disability often have developmental delays and do not progress at the same rate as a non-disabled child of the same age. A child without a disability might learn to walk around a year old. These timeframes are unique to the individual. The same goes for potty-training; it is not unusual for a child with a disability to not be fully potty-trained until much later in life. We spoke about the behaviors of our children, but also the insensitive comments from people such as, "Why aren't they potty-trained?" or "Look how they are acting in the store." This group was just what we needed in many seasons of life, but particularly when Candace later had to have heart surgery. Between that and my church family, we had such an amazing community of support. We did life together.

EIGHT

THE HEART OF THE MATTER

2 Corinthian 5:7
"For we live by faith, not by sight."

The Specially Wrapped Gifts Encouragement group was just what the doctor ordered. This group was not just about being the person that would provide support and have all the answers. It was also about admitting I too needed encouragement.

Candace was born with two separations in her heart. According to the Centers for Disease Control, 50% of all babies born with Down Syndrome have a congenital heart defect. One separation had already closed up on its own, but the other remained open. We continued to take Candace to her follow-up cardiologist appointments and felt in our hearts that God would close the second one without intervention. The holes in her heart were not causing problems. Candace did not experience shortness of breath and she had never turned blue. As a matter of fact, she was full of energy and was a flyer on a special needs cheerleading team.

I took Candace to one of her follow up appointments and the second separation had not closed, so her doctor recommended open-heart surgery. Candace was only four years old at the time. I called Bruce crying while still at the doctor's office because I felt devastated. We scheduled another appointment right away so we could have time to come up with questions and hopefully, other options besides open-heart surgery. Knowing that she would have a permanent scar bothered me and I found myself grieving for Candace. *She is just a baby—not open-heart surgery!* She would have a scar that would be a constant reminder. In my anguish, I thought if I could I would have gladly traded places with her—*this is not fair.* The doctor said as she got bigger the scar would get smaller and recommended that surgery truly was the best course of action. He said the best time to close it was right then and reminded us that the surgery could help eliminate problems for her later on in life. Bruce and I struggled with this option because we could not see anything outwardly wrong with Candace. She appeared to be healthy and thriving, so we were not alarmed about anything. The doctor understood our concern but said because they knew it was there, they should correct it. We agreed to move forward with the surgery but continued to pray, research, and seek second opinions. Candace's surgery was scheduled for July 2013. She was four and a half years old, and the surgery was to take place at Vanderbilt Children's Hospital in Nashville, Tennessee.

We tried to make arrangements at the Ronald McDonald House, but they fell through, so we priced hotel reservations. We were not familiar with the layout of where we were going but trusted God along the way that He would provide. One Sunday after church, a fairly new family to our congregation got wind of Candace's story because we were praying, and our church family was praying for her healing. They approached my husband and said they had vacation points they wanted us to use to book our hotel stay in Nashville for our daughter's surgery. We were so grateful, especially because the hotel was in close proximity to Vanderbilt. God showed us His provision through our loving church family.

We decided that Cherie would travel with us. We had friends in Nashville that would take her out to the park and spend time with their kids who were around her age, so she would not be cooped up in the hospital. My family would arrive later in the week. The day before surgery we met with the doctor. I was still hopeful that just in time, God had answered, performed a miracle, and she would tell us the hole in Candace's heart had closed. I did not want her to have to go through this, but that was not what the doctor said, and surgery was still scheduled for the following day. I wished that I could take her place.

Leading up to Candace's surgery, we had spent time fasting and praying for healing. One particular passage that spoke to me was Genesis 22 when God tested Abraham with his son Isaac. My hope was that God would just say, "she's healed" and she would not have to go through this. Instead, His word to me during that time was, "Trust me *more* with Candace." Honestly, these words made me afraid because I did not know what that meant.

What was God going to do in this situation? I continued to pour my heart out in prayer because I was afraid that she was going to die. I grappled with this because I have seen God do the miraculous. So why was he not choosing to do this for Candace? During this journey, I learned that God is the source of all healing, but we as humans may still get frustrated with his methods. Doctors and medications are an extension of His grace. He gives doctors wisdom. Just because He is not healing supernaturally, does not mean that He is not the source for the healing.

To help better understand the procedure that Candace was having, we attended a child life class, where they used a teddy bear so that our family could understand what would happen. Candace's surgery went well, but our hearts broke when we saw her in recovery hooked up to machines and chest tubes in her little body. We were upset, angry, and afraid, but in the small voice of a six-year-old, Cherie reminded us what the doctor said yesterday that this will look bad, but she is okay. Out of the

mouths of babes, as they say! We stayed at
Children's for three days and were released to go
home, but Candace would have to stay in the house
for 30 days and limit visitors. By the end of the
week, she wanted to go outside--Candace is
resilient! During the time of Candace's surgery, she
was a flyer on a special needs cheerleading team that
had been started by high school cheerleaders. The
name of the team was the "Lemon sharks." After her
surgery, we affectionately referred to her scar as her
"shark bite."

Life goes on even when you are in the
hospital. While in Vanderbilt, we met so many
families for which this was routine; they had spent
months in the hospital. I wondered where their
support was. My heart ached for them. We were
blessed to have great support. Family, friends called
to check on us, prepare meals and sent cards. Our
church family was praying around the clock.

Candace continued to do well after her
surgery. The challenge was that as her parents, we
did not see the problem. We had to trust the doctor,

who had a different vantage point in this situation. This has been the theme for our life: learning to walk by faith and not by our feelings, other people's opinions, or only by what we could comprehend. I have learned to trust God at a deeper level, and I could not have had this lesson by reading about it or watching someone else go through it. I had to taste and see the goodness of God for my own life, in Candace's life and our family's life.

At some point, all of us will go through situations that I affectionately call "Specially Wrapped Gifts." These are circumstances that, on the outset, are not what you planned for, but God's providential hand moves, guides, and prompts. He is at work behind the scenes, fitting what seems to be random and coincidental pieces together to tell a beautiful story. In retrospect, that has been our experience: God maneuvering behind the scenes, ordering our steps to get us to the place that He already planned for us. I am a perpetual student, learning to not fight the process but trusting God through it.

In the very beginning, I had concerns about Cherie (I still do!) and how she would fare, having a sibling with special health needs. By the grace of God, she is the most well-rounded young lady I know. I am proud to say, she is not only smart but also a great friend to her peers, sensitive to God's spirit and beautiful inside and out. She has had to grow up quickly but adapts to change and remains stable in her convictions. I think of BJ, who at the completion of this book is in Graduate School studying for his PhD. in Physical Therapy. He is a brilliant young man, with a good head on his shoulders. He is true to his convictions and remains sensitive to the needs of others around him. In retrospect, my fears and concerns were normal. Further along on the journey, I see how it has worked together for good.

Bruce and I have faced challenges, but we have stayed committed to God, each other, and our family. Early in marriage it all about the honeymoon period, you experience the euphoria of love. Through life happenings, you realize what "real love" is "Love is patient, love is kind, love is long-suffering, love keeps no record of wrongs, rejoices in truth, love always hopes and perseveres…Love never fails" (1 Corinthians 13:4-8 paraphrase). I am truly blessed to be the wife and mother of a family affected by disability. I count it a privilege that God would entrust me with this calling. Perhaps, God knows me better than I know myself. There have been times during this journey when I have chuckled to myself and thought, *"You knew the whole time."* I know, of course, He does, He is All-Knowing. When I reflect on how God orchestrated the events in Bruce's and my life to prepare us for our special family, His attention to the details is mind-boggling. We must have God's perspectives on our situations in life. Life is too difficult without it! Having a child with Down Syndrome is a gift that I would not have asked for, but now I see what a beautiful blessing it is. I wouldn't return or exchange this gift for any amount in the whole world.

"Uses the weak things of the world to confound the wise."

I needed to be taught how to be God-like and see others the way God sees them. More than anything I could learn in a textbook, classroom, Sunday school, and any other experience. My lessons on how to live like Christ are taught by Cherie and Candace: to love without conditions. Candace has taught me how to enjoy the moment and be fully present in what I am doing. I feel like she has a sensitivity to the spirit of God that I will never know this side of heaven. The way she instinctively knows when someone needs a hug. She is drawn to people with visible pain and disability. What is interesting is that Candace loves to play with baby dolls and all of hers have a physical disability. She is not affected by labels of the barriers that we (society) have erected. The barriers that prevent us from crossing racial, socioeconomic, disabled boundaries. She sees people the way God sees them. Candace is not fearful to use her gifts and she doesn't give a thought to what other people think. She lives free. A story that I carry with me was the day Candace started Kindergarten and her school bus, the short bus, came to pick her up. She was independent and we felt proud. The short bus, once an object of ridicule and shame was now empowering. Empowering Candace, she now had access to education and for us, the hard work and sacrifices were paying off. We were eyewitnesses to seeing the fruit of our labor.

Where are we now?

Specially Wrapped Gifts Ministry has evolved, primarily because a door opened for me to return to graduate school and pursue my Master of Science in Social Work. With that training, I have been able to do more research, especially on family dynamics as it relates to families affected by special needs. Also, it trained me to be a counselor to assist families in problem-solving, coping and bringing about emotional healing.

One goal that we have is to be able to assist families that have to travel for medical procedures. The second goal is to influence and shape policies that create positive changes for families affected by disability. And finally, we desire to continue to bring hope by breaking the stigma, breaking the shame, and bringing healing.

I have great expectations that society will continue to evolve, and disability will be normalized. One day the gifts and talents of people with disabilities will be fully appreciated and integrated into our society. Churches and communities of faith will be intentional about including families affected by disabilities in their congregation. *Be encouraged!*

AFTERWORD:

THE SPECIAL MOTHER

By Erma Bombeck (1974)

First appeared in her Mother's Day Column

Most women become mothers by accident, some by choice, a few by social pressures and a couple by habit.

This year nearly 100,000 women will become mothers of handicapped children. Did you ever wonder how mothers of handicapped children are chosen? Somehow, I visualize God hovering over earth selecting his instruments for propagation with great care and deliberation. As He observes, He instructs His angels to make notes in a giant ledger.

"Armstrong, Beth; son. Patron saint...give her Gerard. He's used to profanity."

"Forrest, Marjorie; daughter. Patron saint, Cecelia."

"Rutledge, Carrie; twins. Patron saint, Matthew."

Finally, He passes a name to an angel and smiles, "Give her a handicapped child."
The angel is curious. "Why this one God? She's so happy."

"Exactly," smiles God, "Could I give a handicapped child to a mother who does not know laughter? That would be cruel."

"But has she patience?" asks the angel.

"I don't want her to have too much patience or she will drown in a sea of self-pity and despair. Once the shock and resentment wear off, she'll handle it."

"I watched her today. She has that feeling of self and independence that is so rare and so necessary in a mother. You see, the child I'm going to give her has his own world. She has to make him live in her world and that's not going to be easy."

"But, Lord, I don't think she even believes in you."

God smiles, "No matter, I can fix that. This one is perfect -she has just enough selfishness."

The angel gasps – "Selfishness? Is that a virtue?"

God nods, "If she can't separate herself from the child occasionally, she'll never survive. Yes, here is a woman whom I will bless with a child less than perfect.

She doesn't realize it yet, but she is to be envied. She will never take for granted a 'spoken word'.
She will never consider a 'step' ordinary.
When her child says 'Mummy' for the first time, she will be present at a miracle, and will know it!"

"I will permit her to see clearly the things I see...ignorance, cruelty, prejudice....and allow her to rise above them. She will never be alone. I will be at her side every minute of every day of her life because she is doing My Work as surely as if she is here by my side".

"And what about her Patron saint?" asks the angel, his pen poised in mid-air. God smiles, "A mirror will suffice"

REFERENCES

Centers for Disease Control 2018- website

- Caring for Children with Special Healthcare Needs

- Birth Defects- Down Syndrome

Communicating with and about people with disabilities – People First Language
https://www.cdc.gov/ncbddd/disabilityandhealth/pdf/disabilityposter_photos.pdf

Conway, S., & Meyer, D. (2008). Developing support for siblings of young people with disabilities. *Support for Learning*, 23 (3), 113-117.

Individuals with Disabilities Education Act
https://sites.ed.gov/idea/about-idea/

National Down Syndrome Society
https://www.ndss.org/about-down-syndrome/down-syndrome/

Rawson, H. (2009). "I'm going to be here long after you've gone"-sibling perspectives of the future. Journal of Learning Disabilities, 38, 225-231

Swindoll, C. When God's gift Comes Specially Wrapped, Single message. Insight for Living

Tennessee Early Intervention System (TEIS)
https://www.tn.gov/education/early-learning/tennessee-early-intervention-system-teis/teis-eligibility.html

ACKNOWLEDGMENTS

This book is dedicated to my husband and children. Bruce, when we said, "I Do," not only was it a commitment to each other, but I realize even more so, our "I Do's," was a commitment to God. I do, to His plans, purposes, and will for our family. Through it all, you continue to say, "I do," to God and to me. Thank you for your love towards me for always supporting my dreams. You always push me to go for it and encourage me to shine bright. I love you!

To BJ, Cherie, and Candace: thank you all for making my life so special.

To the two most influential women in my life: my mother and grandmother. Thank you for all that you instilled in me and for shaping my character to be the woman I am today.

To my father, thank you for your encouragement and for giving me the gift of laughter.

I have had some great mentors along the way who poured into my life and I'm grateful for each of you. One, in particular, Joy, my prayer partner, and friend. You are truly missed.

ABOUT THE AUTHOR

Shemeka Cherry Jackson, LMSW, is the founder of Specially Wrapped Gifts Ministry, wife, mother, and advocate for families affected by special health needs and/or disabilities (and so much more!). She was born and raised in Chicago, Illinois. Shemeka is a Navy Veteran, received her Bachelor of Arts in Psychology with a minor in Women's

Studies from the University of Illinois at Chicago. She has a Master's degree in Social Work from the University of Tennessee Knoxville and is a member of Phi Alpha National Social Work Honor Society and SALUTE Honor Society for Veterans.

Shemeka currently resides in Knoxville, TN with her husband Bruce and their two daughters, Cherie and Candace. She enjoys reading, listening to podcasts, and spending time laughing with family and friends.

Specially Wrapped Gifts, (SWG), is a 501(c)(3) non-profit registered in the State of Tennessee. Our mission is to demonstrate the love of Christ to families affected by Special Health Needs and/or Disabilities by providing encouragement and resources.